DEVIL'S ADVOCATE

Donald Freed

BROADWAY PLAY PUBLISHING INC
New York
www.broadwayplaypublishing.com
info@broadwayplaypublishing.com

The play was first published by B P P I in September 2003 in the collection *Plays By Donald Freed Volume 2*
Cover image by Stuart Patterson for Colorola
First printing this edition: October 2011
I S B N: 978-0-88145-502-1
Book design: Marie Donovan
Page make-up: Adobe Indesign
Typeface: Palatino
Printed and bound in the U S A

CHARACTERS & SETTING

THE GENERAL, *Manuel Antonio Noriega, deposed dictator of Panama*

THE ARCHBISHOP, *Monsignor José Sebastian Laboa, the Vatican's ambassador to Panama*

Time: Christmas Eve, 1989

Place: The Vatican Embassy, Panama City, Panama

(Setting: The large, spartan, whitewashed room on the second story of the papal residence in Panama City. There is a desk, a table, telephone, a cot, a small stove, a ceiling fan.)

(On the wall is a large photograph of Pope John Paul II, and a fifteenth century crucifix; on the other, a painting of the "Liberator" Simon Bolivar.)

(Most of the back wall, center, is a large door-window that gives onto a balcony. There is a lavatory, Left, and the double-door entrance is Right. The front or fourth wall is also a double window.)

(A mélange of sounds in the dark: voices, Ronald Reagan and George H W Bush, gunfire, bombs, sirens...)

(In the darkness, the embassy bells strike six. A helicopter zooms in and out. Sirens wail in the distance, moving closer, there is a scattered rifle fire.)

(The long and wide rear door-window is open, the sky glows red with the setting sun. The bloody light creeps in illuminating the spare white room. The last rays catch a kneeling figure, center: Monsignor Laboa. The grey Vatican troubleshooter is in his seventies, and at the height of his spiritual powers—though he is a dying man, and knows it.)

(The Nuncio is a Basque from Northern Spain and a former Vatican "Devil's Advocate" whose role at Rome was to act as the Grand Inquisitor, \whose tribunal investigated reports of miracles and the canonization of new saints. As the Abogado del Diablo, *it was the Archbisop's charge to cut to shreds all impostors and false miracles.)*

(The blood-red rays of sunset spill over the ARCHBISHOP'*s white tropical shirt and dark crucifix.)*

(His eyes are closed as he prays. Helicopters and sirens rise, then fade. The temperature rises above 100 degrees.)

(Suddenly, framed in the double doors stands the GENERAL*: Manual Antonio Noriega: early fifties, powerful, with a pock-marked face.)*

(He is sweaty and covered with grime, wearing Bermuda shorts and a torn grey v-necked T-shirt. Smoke actually rises from his shoes, clothes and hair. He holds in his hands an Uzi machine pistol. The ARCHBISHOP *continues to pray, lips moving, as the* GENERAL *pants and stares. At length:)*

GENERAL: ...Excellency.

(The ARCHBISHOP *stops, opens his eyes, turns his head. The stink of the fugitive hits the priest. The* ARCHBISHOP *and the* GENERAL *stare at each other. Battle sounds from outside rise and fall.)*

ARCHBISHOP: ...General. You came. Come in.

(The GENERAL *does not move. Sounds of vehicles outside, below, then a P A system crackling to life)*

P A: ...Stand-by... *(Static)* Operation "Just Cause" is victorious. The legal and legitimate government of Panama *(Static)* the democratically elected *(Static)* The capture of Narcodictator Manuel Antonio Noriega... The monster is hiding in the papal residence condemned by the whole world *(Static)* an international gangster *(Static)* a pariah and traitor by the Organization of the American States and fugitive from justice for the murder of Panamanian patriot Doctor Hugo Spadafora *(Static)* Stand-by stand-by... Hugo Spadafora...

(Static, then silence. The ARCHBISHOP *makes the sign of the cross.)*

ARCHBISHOP: Hugo Spadafora.

GENERAL: My only friend.

ARCHBISHOP: Your closest friend. Lord have mercy on his soul; Christ have mercy on him. Won't you come in.

(The GENERAL *is frozen, but bluffs valiantly.)*

GENERAL: Amen. Pray for *him*... Don't pray for me, Holiness.

(Sound of gunfire)

GENERAL: Pray for them! Ah-ha-ha-ha! Listen to it, *listen* to it—they're finished, Nuncio. Finished!

ARCHBISHOP: Who is? Come in, sir.

GENERAL: The Yankees, the gringos, they're finished. Because "I Shall Return!" *(He collapses with silent laughter, gasping for air.)*

ARCHBISHOP: I don't understand. Please enter and sit down, you're—

GENERAL: MacArthur, General MacArthur— "I Shall Return!"—Pray for *them*!

(The ARCHBISHOP *tries to rise, but cannot.)*

ARCHBISHOP: You're exhausted, sir. The heat, the smoke—

(The ARCHBISHOP *gestures, again, for the fugitive to enter, but the* GENERAL *still clings to the door frame.)*

GENERAL: Listen, Nuncio, I can get asylum anywhere in the world, now, anywhere!

ARCHBISHOP: But I've been waiting—you promised that if—

GENERAL: But only if, uh...

ARCHBISHOP: In the last resort. Exactly. This would be your sanctuary. I would be your liaison.

GENERAL: No, I know I promised, but now the Yankees have bombed an open city—on Christmas Eve!—like the Nazis in Spain, you remember—

ARCHBISHOP: Please—the heat—I am not well today—can you, ah?

(*The* ARCHBISHOP *holds out his hand, asking for help, to stand—this forces the* GENERAL *to step slowly into the room. The priest, as he rises painfully, clings to the outlaw.*)

ARCHBISHOP: Ah, thank you. Your shoes seem to be, ah, smoking, General.

(*The monster starts to move back, but the* ARCHBISHOP *grasps the* GENERAL'*s hand with all his strength. The* GENERAL *stares at the priest—sways, knows that he has been caught—for the moment. Pause. The priest seizes the temporary advantage, and leads Noriega to a chair.*)

ARCHBISHOP: Thank you, thank you—now, please sit, *Commandante.*

GENERAL: I can stand.

ARCHBISHOP: Please.

(*The* GENERAL *draws on his remaining strength to, literally, put the* ARCHBISHOP *into the chair—tucking him down, covering over with words his own disastrous condition.*)

GENERAL: This is the end of "due process," the end of North American "democracy," the finish for all their Anglo-Saxon *habeus corpus* hocus pocus!

ARCHBISHOP: General—

GENERAL: I am a "Prisoner of War" —and I shall return! (*He sinks to his knees.*)

ARCHBISHOP: Don't talk for a minute, General.

GENERAL: They tried to drive me crazy—so I'd hide deep in the swamps where they could starve me out but I escaped and I'm here and I'm driving *them* crazy.

I want you to tell the media—I want you to make a statement—I want...I want....

ARCHBISHOP: Shh, General, shh, just a moment.

GENERAL: Tell them! Tell C N N! *(He is sinking, collapsing, fighting to stay conscious.)*

ARCHBISHOP: Tell "who" "what," General?

GENERAL: To Fidel Castro they only sent exploding cigars—fuck me! —But *me, me,* they invade a country to make a "drug bust"!-they bomb an open city, they kidnap a head of state! *(He finally runs out of voice. The heat is intense.)* And all because I told Ronald Reagan to "kiss my black ass" when he wanted to use Panama to invade Nicaragua!

ARCHBISHOP: A drink of water?

GENERAL: *(Sinking)* Father-the sneak attack, like Pearl Harbor, on an open city, on Christ's birthday!

(The GENERAL tries to make the sign of the cross. The ARCHBISHOP suppresses a bitter laugh at this brazen display, then also crosses himself. A pause. A whisper)

GENERAL: Like the Nazis in Spain—you are a Basque, Father, you understand *Guernica!* Picasso had Basque blood—like you. *Guernica! (He holds onto the priest's shoulder, as he makes a pathetic simulation of Picasso's agonized horse.)*

ARCHBISHOP: Steady.

GENERAL: I need....

ARCHBISHOP: Yes.

GENERAL: Need...

ARCHBISHOP: ...The lavatory? Follow me.

(The GENERAL is lost in his trance. He cannot move. The priest leads the half mad, half staggering GENERAL into the lavatory, Left, and closes door. The P A squawks to life

again. The ARCHBISHOP *emerges and watches from both the U S and D S double windows.)*

P A: ...Operation "Just Cause" has restored democracy to the Isthmus... *(Static)* The butcher, Noriega, the narcoterrorist... *(Static)* has been trapped like a rat inside the Papal Embassy. The dictator has been indicted for narcotrafficking and the murder of Dr Hugo Spadafora... *(Static)* Panama is free! ...Stand by for an important announcement... Panama is free, Democracy has been restored, Panama is a free country once again! God bless Operation "Just Cause," God Bless Panama, God bless the U S A! *(A few G Is sing out a weak chorus of cheers. The P A sputters out. In the lavatory, water runs.)*

(The ARCHBISHOP *goes to the telephone and speaks to an aide; he plays with a cigarette and lighter constantly; his voice is, now, no longer sick and old. It is steel.)*

ARCHBISHOP: ...Yes. Send up the supper tray; one bottle of beer, *one.* And tell them: stay out; do not come in: no matter what they hear, no matter what I may say or do—or not do. These are my final orders. Disconnect this instrument... Yes. *Now. (He hangs up.)*

(The GENERAL *emerges—seemingly a new man—barefoot from the bathroom, in a bulky robe, towel in hand. The two men study each other. The ectomorphic Inquisitor from the Vatican, and the endomorphic Dictator from the Third World gutter of hell.)*

(The GENERAL *still carries his weapon. It is almost dark. He walks through the shadows to the windows U S and D S—stares and laughs.)*

GENERAL: Mussolini!

ARCHBISHOP: Pardon?

GENERAL: Mussolini.

ARCHBISHOP: Shh... No.

(The GENERAL *laughs and joins the* ARCHBISHOP.)

GENERAL: No... *(Whispers)* Holiness, when we spoke on the telephone—

ARCHBISHOP: Some time ago, yes, but, ah, I'm afraid we've been overtaken by events, and ah—

GENERAL: No, listen, I told you then, and I tell you now, that I will never be taken alive by—

(The ARCHBISHOP *suddenly lifts his voice, points to the overhead fan and speaks as if to a listening device. The* GENERAL *reacts with deep suspicion.)*

ARCHBISHOP: General—I am acting, here, as a "good office" for both the United States of America and the Organization of American States— *(He turns on the lights.)*

GENERAL: No! They're watching. *(Points to the fan, whispers)* That's the American "bug."

ARCHBISHOP: Mm. It used to be yours.

(Both men try here, and often, to make each other smile or laugh—as a sign of mutual humanity.)

GENERAL: ...Watching and listening. Any pretext to kill me. *(He turns off the lights.)*

ARCHBISHOP: You are safe here, sir, as if you were in the Vatican, itself.

GENERAL: ...That's what I'm afraid of. That "bug" was originally *yours.*

ARCHBISHOP: ...You make a little joke. I only serve here.

GENERAL: I beg your pardon. A bad joke... It's madness out there. Those people—the ones they're bombing— loved the U S—when Jimmy Carter came here they turned out three hundred thousand strong to cheer him—am I lying?

ARCHBISHOP: No. *(Pointing)* There is our photograph: the two of us with the President.

GENERAL: Their children in their arms...And you and I on the red carpet. *(He tries to sing* Hail to the Chief—*staggers.)*

ARCHBISHOP: Sit down... You warned President Carter, that day. "Watch your back," you whispered in his ear.

GENERAL: ...He's gone.

ARCHBISHOP: Yes.

GENERAL: And I'm a dead man, and—

ARCHBISHOP: No.

GENERAL: You, Holiness, are the only one left standing.

ARCHBISHOP: For the moment... Sit down now, rest. You need, ah, food, you need—

GENERAL: I need Kiki.

ARCHBISHOP: Your public relations liaison that, ah-

GENERAL: My mistress... They hanged Mussolini with his mistress, didn't they?

ARCHBISHOP: *(Shrugs)* The Italians.

GENERAL: By the heels. Upside down. *Non bella figura.*

ARCHBISHOP: The Americans—the North Americans are different.

GENERAL: Sure. They hang you by the balls—forgive me, Your Grace.

(The ARCHBISHOP *and the* GENERAL *laugh.)*

ARCHBISHOP: *Si.*

GENERAL: Without your mistress.

ARCHBISHOP: *Si.*

GENERAL: Alone.

(The GENERAL *stares into space. The* ARCHBISHOP *circles behind him, slowly, measuring him as a hunter would his prey.)*

ARCHBISHOP: *(Softly)* Food... Eat...

GENERAL: Hm? Food? The "Last Supper." Hmm... When I came in—were you praying for me?

(The ARCHBISHOP *avoids the question by lighting a cigarette, which triggers a spasm of coughing.)*

GENERAL: You're still smoking? It'll kill you, Ambassador.

(The GENERAL *gestures with his gun, then smiles with the ambassador, and puts the Uzi down on the cot.)*

GENERAL: You never believed I would come to you for sanctuary? You thought I was dead already?—You hoped I was dead?

ARCHBISHOP: No, General. I was not even here.

(The GENERAL *leans on a table. Teasing, testing, watching.)*

GENERAL: No, you were on your "holiday".

ARCHBISHOP: I was.

GENERAL: In Guernica.

ARCHBISHOP: Nearby.

GENERAL: In Bilbao... Oh, I know. And you know that I know.... You came back to help me?

ARCHBISHOP: ...I came back.

GENERAL: To help me? *(Silence)* True? No?...Then, why?

(The ARCHBISHOP *crosses to the* GENERAL, *softly.)*

ARCHBISHOP: Your daughters.

(The GENERAL *suddenly sobs, silently. Shaking, he drops his head on the* ARCHBISHOP's *chest. Then, the* GENERAL *pushes away, violently.)*

GENERAL: You are not a father, Father! So don't play that card with me! I will die for my children.

ARCHBISHOP: But will you live for them?

GENERAL: Is that why you came back here, from Guernica, to save my daughters?... No. *(Now he whispers in the priest's face.)* They told you to come back.... From your holiday. *(Whispering)* There's no holiday for you, Father. You went home to die. Don't say a word. I know. Don't speak. You came back. I'm here. You're here.

(The ARCHBISHOP starts to answer, stops; tries to light a cigarette, stops, sits. In the street a burst of gunfire. Then, silence.)

GENERAL: ...So you will feed me and, uh, "protect" me.

ARCHBISHOP: Whatever you need, *Commandante. (He lights another cigarette—coughs and recovers.)* I'm an "addict"... A fair trial: the United States guarantees it.

GENERAL: A fair trial first—then they hang me!

ARCHBISHOP: In Miami, they say anything is possible— in a trial.

GENERAL: Except a miracle! Except justice—anything except justice!

(At the window sirens wailing)

GENERAL: This—is what Reagan—and Bush wanted me to do for them—in Nicaragua.

(The ARCHBISHOP and the GENERAL stare at each other.)

ARCHBISHOP: In North America, you would be on television.

GENERAL: With this face—they would lynch me!

ARCHBISHOP: You would be the ah, the ah—

GENERAL: *(Laughing)* The "underdog"! Ha! Your holiness, you the gray fox, say that to me with a sober face? Did you see me on *60 Minutes*—it was a scandal!

ARCHBISHOP: General, as you say, we are both men of the world.

GENERAL: Absolutely—that is why I came here—because you are a man of this world and the next.

(The ARCHBISHOP *and the* GENERAL *both laugh, then stop at the implication: the "next world" —Hell—is here, now, opening at their feet. The priest looks away into the pit; dizzy, he sits.)*

GENERAL: *(Continuing)* When I first met you—1978?

ARCHBISHOP: Ahh...1977. I have these dizzy spells.

GENERAL: 1977. You were still the Grand Inquisitor in the Vatican,you were—

ARCHBISHOP: "Grand Inquisitor" is only a title, it's not—

GENERAL: The *Abogado del Diablo*, the "Devil's Advocate". It was you who decided which miracles were authentic.

(They laugh.)

GENERAL: Yes, and who qualified as a saint.

ARCHBISHOP: I'm just another bureaucrat.

GENERAL: *(Smiling)* My name never came up, did it—for sainthood?

ARCHBISHOP: No. Not during my tour of duty. Perhaps higher up.

GENERAL: No. No! Don't be too modest. You tore all liars to shreds. You were famous. That's why I came here.

ARCHBISHOP: *(Pause)* Why?

GENERAL: So you could judge—whether I was a "saint" —or not—or whether I was the Devil, like the Yankees say.

ARCHBISHOP: Is that why you came?

GENERAL: No—no, no—ha, ha! —I came here so that we could go to Spain together. I love Barcelona, you go back to Bilbao. We will visit each other and talk about the good old days...I'll be on your doorstep—with a ham from San Sebastian.

ARCHBISHOP: Umm... Perhaps... Is it to be Spain, then?

GENERAL: Don Quixote and, ah, yours truly, eh?

(The ARCHBISHOP's *and the* GENERAL's *smiles fade. Silence. A discreet rap outside the door. The* GENERAL *stiffens, rises for his gun. The* ARCHBISHOP *goes to the door, steps into the corridor and returns with a tray of food.)*

ARCHBISHOP: ...I'm going to cook a special dish for you.

GENERAL: Spanish?

ARCHBISHOP: No, Basque... Then you will tell me—man to man—why you came.

GENERAL: Or you will tell me.... I see that there is enough food for two....But of course, you were expecting me.

(The ARCHBISHOP's *and the* GENERAL's *eyes meet. The* ARCHBISHOP *turns to the hotplate to prepare the food. The P A blasts out from below.)*

P A: *(Static)* ...The narcotyrant is hiding under the skirts of the Papal Nuncio—*(Static)* stand trial as war criminal *(Static)* worse than Hitler and Stalin *(Static)* war criminal *(Static)* narcotraffic and the murder of Hugo Spadafora... Operation "Just Cause" — *(Static)* Pineapple Face has been hunted down by the people of Panama *(Static)* betrayed by the pock-marked Pineapple Face— *(Static)*

(The ARCHBISHOP *throws up his hands and closes the big door-window. The blast drops but still penetrates. From time to time the* GENERAL *laughs. Searchlights cross back and forth outside the window.)*

P A: ...millions of dollars' worth of cocaine have been discovered in the narcoterrorist's quarter— *(Static)*

GENERAL: *(Roaring)* Tamale flour! Tamale dough!

P A: ...evidence of the dreaded witchcraft *Santeria!* Blood, both human and chicken— *(Static)*

GENERAL: Hot sauce! Tabasco!

P A: And red underwear! The red underwear of a *Santeria* Witch!

(The GENERAL *erupts in sustained silent laughter. The* ARCHBISHOP *holds his ears and tries to cook.)*

GENERAL: Red underwear—Hitler's red underwear—no, *Stalin's red underwear!*

(Silence, again. The priest cooks and watches. The tyrant fights to remain conscious.)

GENERAL: Mm—you said, uh, the Basque men, they?—

ARCHBISHOP: Can cook! Yes, *commandante.* The male population is divided into gastronomic clubs, every week your club meets and the members....

(The nuncio sees that the monster is fighting to keep his eyes open. The priest takes a tablet for his heart. The GENERAL *twitches and moans, the priest studies him... The* ARCHBISHOP *makes a stealthy move toward the window. The* GENERAL *opens an eye to spy on him. A siren screams past in the street, the* GENERAL *staggers to his feet, the priest resumes his soothing cooking talk.)*

ARCHBISHOP: *(Continuing)* ...Yes, no women allowed.

GENERAL: Huh?

ARCHBISHOP: In the eating clubs.

GENERAL: Oh. No... What's that?

ARCHBISHOP: Here. I'll show you.... This mushroom we call the Paradillo. We sauté it in a little olive oil with a little garlic and parsley.... Mix the eggs with this Idiazabal cheese, made from ewe's milk... Stir for a moment, I'll set the table. *(He sets a place for one.)*

GENERAL: This is not like the food you had at my house.... Your Basque "eating clubs" were a "front" for something else—no?

ARCHBISHOP: Not that I ever knew.

GENERAL: I am talking about many years ago, when you, ah, when the young revolutionaries organized your "eating clubs" with a certain "menu" in mind, mm?

(From the P A a martial anthem, and the clanging of pots and pans. Both men rush to peer out the window, then suddenly, the window lights up a fiery red. The ARCHBISHOP stalks to the door.)

ARCHBISHOP: They're burning down the trees in the park. Has everyone gone mad!?

(The GENERAL leaps for his gun. The ARCHBISHOP stiffens. The window is a sheet of red flame.)

GENERAL: They're burning the trees so that they can land Green Berets there—to storm this embassy! *(He cocks his gun.)* Get back—get down!

ARCHBISHOP: They will not dare—unless you force them, General!

GENERAL: *(He pushes the ARCHBISHOP to the wall.)* Get down—get back—"force" them! That's a goddamn death squad out there and they're coming in! Have you got a gun, Archbishop?!

ARCHBISHOP: General—give me your gun before they—

GENERAL: Never! Listen, Holiness, they have invaded an entire country and killed thousands of people to arrest one man—me!

ARCHBISHOP: Put it down! This is holy ground. I am going out there—to tell them that I have granted you sanctuary. They cannot and will not enter the sacred premises.

GENERAL: We are going to die, Father—you and me—within the hour! I want my uniform, my full uniform—I refuse to die in a bathrobe!

ARCHBISHOP: Stay here!

(The ARCHBISHOP *turns on his heel and leaves...The* GENERAL *crouches at the window, with his machine pistol. The din builds. The* GENERAL's *lips twist and mutter, then—silence...Then a building-shaking explosion of rock and roll: "Drug Busters!" He runs to the telephone, finds it dead, rips it out.)*

GENERAL: *(Screams at the window)* Cocksucker!... Cunts!... Faggots!

(The beat builds, the walls shake. The GENERAL *roars and dances to the music, singing and cursing. In total rebellion he pulls open the big windows. Suddenly, the blast stops, and his laughter rings out in silence. The* ARCHBISHOP *re-enters and closes the window. The* GENERAL *subsides. Pause)*

ARCHBISHOP: They stopped.

GENERAL: Psychological Warfare.

ARCHBISHOP: For now.

GENERAL: Their plan is to drive me crazy.

ARCHBISHOP: But you will not give them the satisfaction, will you?

(Pause)

GENERAL: What did you tell them?

ARCHBISHOP: That the refugees on the ground floor could not survive such torture.

GENERAL: What refugees—on the ground floor?

ARCHBISHOP: The others who have been granted asylum.

GENERAL: Who?

ARCHBISHOP: Well, let's see: there is your military chaplain who barely escaped from a whorehouse, and there is—

(The GENERAL begins to laugh.)

ARCHBISHOP: There is the Director of the Bank of Panama who embezzled thirty million, with his wife and children and, ah, "nanny"; your Minister of Health whose office contained a cocaine laboratory, four torturers and three murderers from your "Dignity Battalion": two Peruvian terrorists; and, ah, one Cuban.

GENERAL: Not to mention three Basque fugitives!

ARCHBISHOP: One minute... The Basque men you refer to, ah, they are men from San Sebastian—

GENERAL: Your hometown.

ARCHBISHOP: Yes...

GENERAL: I know.

ARCHBISHOP: And they, ah, are—

GENERAL: Political fugitives from Generalissimo Franco.

ARCHBISHOP: Precisely.

GENERAL: Who has been dead for fifteen years. What a revolutionary you might have been, Father!

(Both men laugh freely. Pause. The ARCHBISHOP *finishes cooking and serves the* GENERAL, *who falls to eating like a man starving. The* ARCHBISHOP *observes.)*

GENERAL: ...Ummm...God... Good... Aah...Basque.

ARCHBISHOP: Basque.

GENERAL: Franco is dead as a dog.

ARCHBISHOP: Amen.

GENERAL: ...You're not eating.

(The nuncio brings more food.)

ARCHBISHOP: ...Go ahead, please... You're ravenous— eat, eat!

GENERAL: ...Three days... Running... Hiding...

ARCHBISHOP: Eat.

GENERAL: ...Like a wild animal.

(Sounds of chants from the street. Sirens. The nuncio goes to the window.)

ARCHBISHOP: ...No, no, it's nothing. A few demonstrators.

GENERAL: What color?

ARCHBISHOP: I beg your pardon?

GENERAL: What color are they?

ARCHBISHOP: Mm—hard to say, hard to see. Not too many.

GENERAL: C I A street mobs, a dollar a dozen.

ARCHBISHOP: Are they?... Finish this bread, please.

(The chanting fades out.)

GENERAL: Not my people.

ARCHBISHOP: No?

GENERAL: Nooo—the real people are in the street fighting the *gringos.*

ARCHBISHOP: There's a report that, ah, looting and burning, rather than fighting, is the order of the day, ah, of the night.

(The ARCHBISHOP *and the* GENERAL *both chuckle.)*

GENERAL: Urban guerilla warfare. I'm serious—my invention.

ARCHBISHOP: ...And your "Dignity Battalions", are they still loyal to you?

GENERAL: Absolutely. To the last man—they're in charge of looting.... *(He turns sober, grim.)* They bombed the barrio—the U S—the barrio is burning.

(The ARCHBISHOP *makes the sign of the cross. The* GENERAL *mops his plate. Then the prisoner cleans up his dining area.)*

ARCHBISHOP: You must rest—you must try—the heat—

(The tyrant stands, swaying with exhaustion, growling.)

GENERAL: ...Stealth bombers, flame throwers...burning bodies...ten thousand homes destroyed in the El Chorrillo section alone—

ARCHBISHOP: Lie down, now—it is over a hundred degrees.

GENERAL: The poorest of the poor—laser weapons—

ARCHBISHOP: Stretch out.

(The tyrant sinks down on the cot.)

GENERAL: No pity—the U S has no pity—laser guns—in San Miguelito melting people—

ARCHBISHOP: Sleep.

GENERAL: No pity...

(The GENERAL *breathes heavily, snoring. The* ARCHBISHOP *turns off all the lights.)*

ARCHBISHOP: Sleep well, sir. *(Silence. He lights a candle and makes a signal at the dark window.)*

GENERAL: ...Wait, Father... My wife...Felicidad...

ARCHBISHOP: Is she safe?

GENERAL: She is with my daughters....

ARCHBISHOP: Close your eyes, General, for an hour or two.

GENERAL: Wait—don't go—my wife's a helluva woman—she tried to kill Kiki—

ARCHBISHOP: I know. She is Spanish, very proud. Do you have a message for her?

GENERAL: ...Tell me about the Basques.

ARCHBISHOP: Not tonight.

GENERAL: My daughters.

ARCHBISHOP: Shhh.

(The ARCHBISHOP *and the* GENERAL *talk in the near-dark like a parent and an overwrought and exhausted child.)*

GENERAL: You told my daughters a story about the Pyrenees mountains—when you visited us at the beach house.

ARCHBISHOP: Your daughters are charming. What shall I tell them?

GENERAL: The story...

ARCHBISHOP: What story?

GENERAL: It's so dark, now.

ARCHBISHOP: Ahh...I told them, didn't I?, about our great mountain, the Pyrenees, that no-one could cross.

GENERAL: Pyrenees.

ARCHBISHOP: Pyrenees. No one can ever cross—to conquer the Basque people.

(The GENERAL *chuckles like a child.)*

ARCHBISHOP: No one could touch us—not for fifty thousand years. Not since the Stone Age. "I am fifty thousand years old—" I told your daughters.

(The GENERAL *laughs with pleasure.)*

ARCHBISHOP: Shh. Rest. You need a bedtime story. You and your girls... So if I am a fifty thousand year old Basque, and I have seen lions with teeth like knives, and woolly elephants, and—

GENERAL: And tigers and—

ARCHBISHOP: Everything, everything, the Basque people have seen every kind of animal, but we were not afraid.

GENERAL: No?

ARCHBISHOP: Shh. No. No need to fear now. Shhh.

GENERAL: Not afraid of "Man"?

ARCHBISHOP: ...No.

GENERAL: My daughters are.

ARCHBISHOP: I know. That is when I told them about Saint Ignatius de Loyola and the Society of Jesus. And then, they were not afraid.... Sleep, now, son.

GENERAL: ...Saint Ignatius was a Basque.

ARCHBISHOP: Yes.

GENERAL: And he saw Christ...

(Silence. Moonlight. The ARCHBISHOP *lifts his face in agony, as if to God, his lips moving in silent prayer. Then he starts to tip-toe out.)*

GENERAL: Wait—stay! Put the lights on! It's too quiet.

ARCHBISHOP: General—don't you trust me?

GENERAL: What?... I ate your food, didn't I?

ARCHBISHOP: You are my guest, sir, I'm a priest.

GENERAL: No—you're a Jesuit.

ARCHBISHOP: Well?

GENERAL: The Jesuits... Today either they join the Revolution or they....

ARCHBISHOP: What?

GENERAL: They're not human.

ARCHBISHOP: They're not?

GENERAL: Not the old-fashioned kind. You know what I'm saying?

ARCHBISHOP: Mm... It's true, when we were the "advanced guard", they drew and quartered us in London—disemboweled us in Ethiopia. We were eaten alive by Red Indians—flayed, drowned, starved, beheaded, bestialized, crucified....

GENERAL: Those were the days, huh, Father?

ARCHBISHOP: Mm... Sleep a little, now, General.

GENERAL: No!-We're going to settle this tonight. (*He jumps up, turns on the lights, confronts the ambassador.*) There's a gringo in the building! Am I right?

ARCHBISHOP: There is a man downstairs in my office.

GENERAL: I knew it!

ARCHBISHOP: How? How did you know it?

GENERAL: I can smell Yankees—through the walls.

ARCHBISHOP: ...I wanted you to eat and rest, before... before you gave me your decision.

GENERAL: ...My decision?

ARCHBISHOP: ...Your choice.

GENERAL: What?

(The ARCHBISHOP *speaks loudly up toward what must be a hidden listening device. The* GENERAL *makes a vulgar gesture toward the ceiling "bug".)*

ARCHBISHOP: Sir—I am acting as a "good office" here tonight for the United States and—

GENERAL: And the Vatican? —Say it, Ambassador!

ARCHBISHOP: And for Western Civilization itself, General.

GENERAL: *Dog shit!* Beg pardon.

(Pause)

ARCHBISHOP: General... What are your orders?

GENERAL: Hmm?

ARCHBISHOP: For the gentleman waiting in my office. He has a direct line to the White House, to President Bush.

GENERAL: What is this "gentleman"'s name?

ARCHBISHOP: Smith.

GENERAL: *(A bark of laughter)* C I A.

ARCHBISHOP: Nevertheless, I must instruct him as to your decision.

GENERAL: About what?

ARCHBISHOP: To stand trial or take sanctuary. Asylum. What foreign embassy you will appeal to for permanent asylum. —But I wanted you to rest before you chose.

(The strongman goes to the window. The red glow is dying. The GENERAL *wipes his head with the towel.)*

GENERAL: It's like hell in here. Can we open it? *(He opens the window. Low sounds.)* ...Spain.

ARCHBISHOP: Spain? That is your choice?

GENERAL: Spain... Or Nicaragua... Or Cuba...

(Suddenly the P A blasts again.)

P A: ...Now hear this. Operation "Just Cause" now
confirms that the narcofiend's secret lair has just been
discovered *(Static)* containing a statue of Hitler; three
hundred Soviet K-34 machine guns; *(Static)* a cache of
voodoo gods; a box of teddy bears; assorted drugs; and
an obscene collection of pornographic paraphernalia—
(Static)

GENERAL: The son-of-a-bitch! Pornography! Telling
people I'm a sex fiend! I know how to play this little
game of "sexpionage" just as good as they can— Bring
that C I A faggot "Smith" up here right now!

ARCHBISHOP: Impossible.

GENERAL: Bring him up! I got a message to give him
for George Herbert Walker Bush. Bring him up. I won't
kill him!

ARCHBISHOP: It's too dangerous, General. You can tell
me and I'll pass it on to him.

GENERAL: *(He pours out a stream of filth into the priest's
ear.)* You can tell him that I have photographs of Willy
Black. Willy Black—Blackie—you know him, the
"Cultural Attache" at the U S Embassy—ha! —I have
Blackie by the balls, I have him on tape, he went to
school with Bush—no, listen—they were in a secret
club, Skull and Bones, together at school and they all—

(The ARCHBISHOP *tries to extricate himself, the* GENERAL
follows him around the room like a snake, hissing in his ear.)

GENERAL: —Blackie swears they were all naked in a big
pool of hot horseshit—listen! This was at Yale, they got
into coffins and took a vow of death—wait! —Blackie
said they—

ARCHBISHOP: Stop! No more!

GENERAL: This is the God's truth and you've heard the same thing in your confessional!

ARCHBISHOP: Gossip! Do not sink to their level.

GENERAL: They all pledged *"Long Live Death!"* — Blackie said, at Yale— "Long live Death!" —like Franco's General—who murdered the Basques! *(He picks up the telephone. His tone is grim.)* It's dead.... Have it connected. Get Bush, himself, on the telephone. Tell him we can deal. Tell him! Tell him I mentioned the word "Yale" —tell him I mentioned the word "Shah"— the word "Hostages"—*the word "Kennedy"!*

ARCHBISHOP: You're shaking, you're ill, you mustn't say such things!

(The GENERAL seizes the ARCHBISHOP in a fierce embrace.)

GENERAL: J F K! Bang. Bang. Bush. Boom, boom. *Comprende!* George Bush—and he's going to order a raid!

ARCHBISHOP: No, not yet...General, tell me about your daughters?... General? General!

GENERAL: No—he's coming—George Herbert Walker Bush—the "wimp" —he who wants to kill "He Who Has The Balls."

ARCHBISHOP: No...Why?

GENERAL: Me and J F K! *Because I know all his secrets!*

(Pause. Then, an overpowering rock'n'roll barrage of You're No Good!*)*

ARCHBISHOP: They must cease this noise!

(The fugitive grabs his crotch and sings out to the Yankees. The priest holds his ears. Then, the music stops. Silence)

GENERAL: ...Once upon a time, we stood here together, eh?

ARCHBISHOP: The passing parade.

GENERAL: President Carter...The Panamanian games.

ARCHBISHOP: '78.

GENERAL: How you loved those games. Especially the wrestling, huh?

ARCHBISHOP: Mmm...

GENERAL: Once upon a time, when you were not yet a novice, when you were piss poor like me, you could have wrestled for Spain—in the Olympics. But you said no.

(The ARCHBISHOP *turns to study the* GENERAL. *A burst of gunfire in the distance then quiet again.)*

GENERAL: A-ha! Do I know you? You were, you could have been, you were that good! —And so was I! *(He begins to shadow box: pawing, snorting, feinting.)* Welterweight champ—I could've been! I had the footwork, I had the jab!

(The inquisitor applauds, encourages the boxer.)

ARCHBISHOP: Bravo! What did they call you?

GENERAL: "El Nino"! "The Kid." *(Boxes)* "El Tigre." *(Boxes)* "Tonito—the kid from Teraplen"—

ARCHBISHOP: Bravo. Bravissimo!

(They laugh and pose like young boys. Suddenly, the music blasts the world apart, again. The ARCHBISHOP *rushes out, his lips moving. The* GENERAL *offers new obscenities to the street then stalks to the lavatory and begins to urinate loudly. The tyrant re-enters from the lavatory holding a drinking glass filled with his own urine. He curses a toast toward the window and the rock'n'roll, and drinks off the "health drink" as the* ARCHBISHOP *re-enters staring in amazement. The rock'n'roll cacophony stops.)*

GENERAL: *Orina.*

ARCHBISHOP: What? No.

GENERAL: *(Sips)* Mmm.

ARCHBISHOP: You make the joke?

GENERAL: It's a health drink...*Orina*... For potency.

ARCHBISHOP: It is?

GENERAL: Natural medicine. *(Toasting)* Victory or Death!

ARCHBISHOP: Well...I have their word.... They will not enter the embassy unless you take me hostage.... So...I have their word, and I have *your* word? Yes? Yes... No, the United States will not permit you to take asylum in Nicaragua or Cuba.... What?

GENERAL: *(A harsh whisper)* ...The United States is the "Evil Empire."

ARCHBISHOP: It's settled.... They *will* permit you to go to Spain.

GENERAL: They will?

ARCHBISHOP: They will.... But Spain refused.

GENERAL: Fucking Spain!

(The GENERAL lunges for his weapon. The ARCHBISHOP sits on it and smiles up at the dictator.)

ARCHBISHOP: I am Basque.

GENERAL: Mexico?

ARCHBISHOP: Ah... They have refused. I'm sorry.

GENERAL: ¡Nos llevo la chingada!— Pardon me, *Padre*.

ARCHBISHOP: *(Shrugging)* The Mexicans...

(The GENERAL looms over the diplomat, then turns away and opens the single bottle of beer. He sits, drinks, thinks. The ARCHBISHOP pours himself a cup of coffee, checks the window, sits. The night sky outside the window is, now, full of stars. Time is passing. Church bells ring. From below

*comes the sound of young people singing "Silent Night" in
sweet medley. The* GENERAL *hums along.)*

ARCHBISHOP: *(Continuing)* Happy Christmas, General.

(The GENERAL *looks at him.)*

ARCHBISHOP: That is why they stopped their, ah,
"music".... But after Christmas Day...

GENERAL: In the morning. A matter of hours. They
will stick it in our ears. I love it. But they will drive *you*
mad.... What is the Vatican saying?

ARCHBISHOP: Very little, except that it is a matter for
the Nuncio, here.

GENERAL: —You?

ARCHBISHOP: Mm...

GENERAL: Do you get the million dollars?

ARCHBISHOP: One million, U S, for capturing the, what
is it? *(Lisping)* The "nasty-Noriega-narconut". No. I
haven't "captured" you.

GENERAL: No...

ARCHBISHOP: In fact, you are a "free man"—in the eyes
of God.

(The GENERAL *puts his gun down on the table between
them.)*

GENERAL: I'm free—to kill myself or surrender to the
U S, let *them* kill me— "legally."

ARCHBISHOP: ...Still, in front of a jury—anything can
happen.

GENERAL: And you will be there to certify that I am a
saint. In Miami?

ARCHBISHOP: No. I will be recalled to Rome.

GENERAL: Why?

(The ARCHBISHOP *smiles.)*

GENERAL: For taking me in? —You can't answer?
—This embassy was supposed to betray me to the
Yankees? Deliver me into the hands of the North
Americans— That's it, isn't it?! —You hate them, too,
don't you?

ARCHBISHOP: I hate only the Devil, and Rock'n'Roll.

(The ARCHBISHOP *and the* GENERAL *smile, sip their drinks,
listen to another Christmas song—the* Ave—*and time
passes.)*

GENERAL: A million dollars, U S, hmm...I could tell the
jury that I'm no saint, but I'm not a witch either.

ARCHBISHOP: True. *(He looks quickly at his watch.)*

GENERAL: And I don't wear red underwear.... But that's
not what they're accusing me of, red underwear and
voodoo magic.

ARCHBISHOP: No.

GENERAL: That's why I'm making you my jury.

ARCHBISHOP: Not me.

GENERAL: And my judge. My jury and my judge. I'm in
your hands. Fire away.

ARCHBISHOP: *(To the listening device)* This is a matter
of international jurisprudence, sir. I am merely a
functionary in this affair. I am not involved.

GENERAL: Archbishop, when Spain took away my only
option, they also took away your only option. So you
are "involved."

ARCHBISHOP: I will never—

GENERAL: —And when they shoot you—and they *will,*
they will blow you away, right along with me—they
will tell the press that I killed *you,* and *they* killed *me.*
That will be the deal—done and done!

ARCHBISHOP: No, they would lose the Catholic vote...
General, I will never betray your asylum—I told you
that when you telephoned me two months ago, I tell
you that tonight. Never; any more than I ever refused
sanctuary to the steady stream of people coming here
to hide, who were running away from *you*. From *you*!

GENERAL: I remember.

ARCHBISHOP: You remember...General, I don't know
whether you wear red underwear or no underwear,
and I don't care. I represent the Holy See here, the
Vatican, the Church Militant.

GENERAL: *(Like a knife thrust, and he draws blood)*
...Didn't you leave out God?

ARCHBISHOP: ...No... Do you want me to hear your
confession?

(If an Act break is desired, it should happen here.)

*(The GENERAL begins to pace in agitation. An organ plays,
far away, in the chapel.)*

GENERAL: What? Hah! Let's open the window, I'm
burning up, let's have some beer!

*(As he reaches the window a helicopter chops in like gunfire.
The GENERAL springs back and away. Chopper out-organ
sound in.)*

ARCHBISHOP: *(The priest lights candles.)* I'm sorry, there
is no more beer.

GENERAL: Torture... Your Reverence, I know that Rome
and Panama City and Washington DC are all cheering
on Operation "Just Cause," and that I am the "cause",
and that your lips are sealed and your hands are tied,
and that the Pope and President are going to kill you to
get to me—when they smash in here on the day after
Christmas—let me make my point—so I'm going to tell
you the truth and you are going to have to judge me,

whether you like it or not! And that is our only chance,
because what happens to me happens to you! The
spooks, the U S spooks, they killed Archbishop Romero
and they will kill you. *Punto.*

(The ARCHBISHOP *turns toward the door, the* GENERAL
moves to the doorway. The organ plays below. The
GENERAL'S *voice is hypnotic: resonating, rumbling,*
whispering.)

GENERAL: Listen Your Holiness, listen: No man can
fool you, you are the Grand Inquisitor, *El Abogado del*
Diablo. You see through all lies and deceit, and that is
why I am going to make you judge me, and if you call
me a liar I swear on my children that I will give myself
up to George Bush—but if you judge me a man—
not a saint—*a man!* and not a monster—if you judge
me that—then! you walk over there to the Spanish
Embassy and tell them that you have found me "not
guilty" and that if Spain does not grant me asylum,
then you are going to the Pope, to the public, to the
President, to the United Nations, to the World—heaven
and earth!

(The organ fugue has reached its apogee, and now drops
out of hearing range. Silence. Church bells. Silence. The
ARCHBISHOP *sits, the* GENERAL *looms over him, behind his*
chair.)

ARCHBISHOP: You are in my hands.

GENERAL: *Si.*

ARCHBISHOP: And I am in yours.

GENERAL: Oh, *si.*

ARCHBISHOP: I cannot judge you, General...I can only
listen to you.

(The GENERAL *turns out the lights except for the candles.*
Then he goes up to the window, where the moonlight frames
him.)

GENERAL: ...The whole truth and nothing but the truth. So help me God...God... Did you know that the Japanese made me a Buddhist. Ha! It's true, there's a statue of me in, uh, somewhere in Japan. The truth... God. In Israel I went to the wailing wall. Israel is fantastic—if I could cut the tip off my prick to meet the laws of circumcision, I'd take asylum in Israel tonight—excuse the language, Your Worship, but we're talking about God here. Of course, I was raised a Catholic and I memorized a whole lot of the old book.

ARCHBISHOP: You're dehydrating, General.

GENERAL: Sweating blood..."I am come to send fire on the earth... And He met a man who was a leper, and the man cried Jesus, Master, have mercy on me, and Jesus said, go show yourself to a priest, and it came to pass, and the leper was cleansed..."

ARCHBISHOP: *(Pause)* The Gospel according to Saint Luke.

GENERAL: "And the leper was cleansed"...Saint Luke... So, I'm an ugly pock-marked son-of-a-bitch but I'm not a witch or a devil.... Not guilty of the first charge..."Go show yourself to a priest."

(Below. The organ begins to play, again.)

(The ARCHBISHOP *has another dizzy spell; breathes, stares at the* GENERAL, *tries to focus. What does he see behind the pock-marks? Moonlight bathes the white room. Sirens far away. The priest studies the prisoner closely. The priest lights a cigarette, the* GENERAL *stubs it out.)*

ARCHBISHOP: You are not a leper. Are you the devil?

GENERAL: ...Eminence—you know me.

ARCHBISHOP: Do I?

GENERAL: But do I know you? *(In the priest's ear)* I know why you went back to Guernica. I know about your "holiday".

ARCHBISHOP: ...It's true, I'm ill.

GENERAL: I know. That's why you went home.... Or is it?

ARCHBISHOP: What? I'm a little deaf.

GENERAL: Your "holiday" was a cover for your illness. It could be that your "illness" was a cover for something else you did in Guernica.

ARCHBISHOP: You would not make a bad Inquisitor yourself, General... You suspect me of helping the Basque terror underground...I hear confessions, General, that's all—confessions.

GENERAL: Me, too. Confessions. But you get yours a different way, huh? Or do you? *(He laughs, rises and paces; slaps himself to stay awake.)* You and I—I mean we helped run this country for the U S, didn't we? "Panama Inc".

ARCHBISHOP: Church and State for the "common good".

GENERAL: That's us. The unholy trinity: the U S and you and me. You "cleansed" souls—I "cleaned" money—and the U S cleaned up!

(The bells toll the hour. The ARCHBISHOP and the GENERAL freeze.)

ARCHBISHOP: Time.

(The GENERAL picks up his gun.)

ARCHBISHOP: What are you doing?

GENERAL: When the cock crows—I'm going to shoot it.... You understand me?

ARCHBISHOP: I think so.

GENERAL: In the garden of Gethsemene—for thirty pieces of silver.

ARCHBISHOP: You think I am Judas Iscariot?

GENERAL: He was the first Jesuit, no?

ARCHBISHOP: If I'm Judas...who are you?

GENERAL: ...You are going to tell me.

ARCHBISHOP: No...There is only time for one confession—before the bells ring for Christmas!

(The GENERAL moves a chair to center and sits like a police prisoner, but holding his gun.)

GENERAL: Go on, start, before they break in. Go on. I'm your prisoner. *(Chuckles)* Torture me!

ARCHBISHOP: You are not guilty of witchcraft of black magic?

GENERAL: No, your Holy Advocate.

ARCHBISHOP: Are you guilty of any crime?

GENERAL: One crime and one crime only: I am guilty of being myself: not Mussolini, not Hitler, Stalin, Castro—no-one but me—I am—I—*ego sum qui sum*—Manual Antonio Noriega! *(He begins to take the gun apart and clean it with his towel.)*

ARCHBISHOP: And who is Manuel Antonio Noriega?

GENERAL: A gorilla—who can read and write.

ARCHBISHOP: ...I'm listening.

(The GENERAL continues to clean his gun in the moon and candlelight. He begins his answer softly and builds slowly.)

GENERAL: Mm...I am the hellspawn of the Cuna tribe—from the Caribbean coast—and the Chocas on the Pacific side. That is my mother, alright?

(The GENERAL glares up at the microphone. Breaks into a kind of savage Cabaret of History. Below, an organ begins

to play a mass. Now the monster begins to work on the
ARCHBISHOP *like a magician taking him deep into the*
myth.)

GENERAL: Now the Conquistadors come in after gold—
they rape and kill—so now you add Spanish scum to
my "Indian" blood, and then you mix that with nigger
slaves that they bring into work after the Indians have
all been made to disappear—you mix in the African
and by that time Columbus has gone mad and died
and Balboa and the rest are rotting in the jungle—but
it goes on—they tear our bodies apart looking for more
gold—

(The GENERAL *begins to stroke his gun. His voice is as*
modulated as the organ playing below—which now ceases.
The ARCHBISHOP *tries to get in a word but the tyrant*
merely winks and points up at the bug in the fan.)

GENERAL: But I survive, in the jungle because I am a
Cimmarone, a runaway slave, a maroon, a wild man of
the swamps. They hunt us, the Spaniards, but we have
become a beast of the jungle. We survive. We hunt
the hunter. We murder and we survive. We mix with
the Carib cannibals, we have poison arrows—we trap
Balboa's last troop in San Sebastian—and-we-eat-them!

ARCHBISHOP: The Spanish.

GENERAL: ...Then Dr-r-rake! And the English came—
because Panama, she has a slim waist and they all want
to fuck her—forgive me, your Honor—in the Isthmus.
So the English came and fucked my mother in the
jungle—pardon me—and I killed *him*, and I survived
in our primeval forest, living on the sloths and the
kinkajous and the possums and the turtles—running
with the pumas and the jaguars and the cougars! *(He*
begins to pace and prowl, as if he were a jaguar, around the
ARCHBISHOP's *chair.)*

ARCHBISHOP: You have lived many lives, General—
now I have the hiccups.

GENERAL: We call our big cats Tigers, one of my old
nick-names: "The Tiger," *El Tigre*.... So, the years rotted
away in the jungle and we man/beasts, we beast/men
spawned and survived.... Until the Yankees, the North
Americans came, and burned down the jungle and
killed our mother for the last time.... But because they
are perverts they fucked her after she was dead—they
plowed a cut, a canal, across her slim waist and the
water ran through her like blood.

(The ARCHBISHOP *tries to make contact, to calm. But the*
GENERAL's *body and voice begin to fill the room.)*

ARCHBISHOP: I'm a Basque, I'm an outsider, I
understand you!

GENERAL: In the zone, Monsignor, in the Canal Zone,
they fucked us in the zone—and now that piece of shit
they call a "treaty" finally gives us control of the Canal
next year, and ownership in 1999—now they declare
war on me so that they can tear up the treaty and
blast a new hole in her— *(Whispering)* using nuclear
explosives to make a bigger canal! *(Face to face, the*
hiccups are frightened away.)

ARCHBISHOP: Keep your voice down, sir, don't push
them too far—wait, let me say a word—it's true,
the United States stole the Panama Canal—fair and
square—please allow me to finish, don't overplay
your hand, sir—It's true, Church and State have
been indicted by history—by "History", General,
not by you, or me, but by the Church itself; she has
apologized to the Jews and someday she will beg the
pardon of Latin America—and so will the United
States—but not today, not tomorrow—the day after
tomorrow, when you and I are gone and not even
pictures on a wall—remembered, dimly, but only if we

do this last thing, together, well—only is we end this affair well, General.

(The GENERAL *talks into the* ARCHBISHOP'*s face.)*

GENERAL: You go downstairs and tell George Bush's fancy boy that I have atomic explosives ready...I have agents in their Military Intelligence, you know that, your Honor. And they'll blow Panama up because there's nothing left of her. They've slashed and burned and raped out the Cuna culture. They use starving white settlers to go in and deforest and deriver—and then after four years, when nothing can grow any more, the white trash moves on to the next virgin forest and in comes the U S agribusiness and takes her from behind—because the U S has cattle and the white trash has only crops and the crops won't grow after four years. Then the chainsaws and the bulldozers—made in the U S A—cut off her breast, the rest of the trees are gone and there's nothing left for the cattle to eat, and then they will blow a nuclear hole right through her.... Tell me that the U S isn't turning that cattle and this whole stinking country into hamburger!

(The ARCHBISHOP *picks up a candle, gestures the* GENERAL *to follow him. He leads the* GENERAL *to the lavatory doorway and runs the water faucet at full. The* ARCHBISHOP *points to the ceiling. His voice is low, he speaks in the* GENERAL'*s ear.)*

ARCHBISHOP: They're listening to everything you say. You know that, don't you?

GENERAL: I know that.

ARCHBISHOP: What the Spanish did, and the English, and the French—you left them out—

GENERAL: *(Mutters)* Fucking French. Forgive me.

(The ARCHBISHOP *and the* GENERAL *whisper in each other's ear. The nuncio grips the* GENERAL.*)*

ARCHBISHOP: All that is "History", now, General.

GENERAL: Genocide.

ARCHBISHOP: "Progress."

GENERAL: Slavery.

ARCHBISHOP: The "Free Market", don't upset yourself.

GENERAL: Starvation.

ARCHBISHOP: Don't take it personally, Commander, it's the price of Civilization and Empire—all empire, holy and unholy.

GENERAL: "Civilization" —and we pay the check!

ARCHBISHOP: And someday the White House and the Vatican will apologize to your great-grandchildren.

GENERAL: (Chuckling) And that is why I have the Canal mined—that's why I'm going to blow it up before they can!

ARCHBISHOP: Shh—listen to me: if you commit a crime like that in the name of the "Past" —you'll be no better than the U S with its, ah, nostalgia for the "Future" — in the name of which they commit their crimes.

GENERAL: (Chortling) I'm going to blow a hole in the Gatun Dam and the Canal will drain into the Atlantic.

ARCHBISHOP: Quiet! ...And they will rebuild it—after they hang you on drug charges—and for murdering your old comrade Hugo Spadafora. Rebuild it with an atomic blast and pave over the rest of the Isthmus and make a super highway between Colombia and Costa Rica.

(The GENERAL lifts his hands to the ARCHBISHOP's throat. The priest gives a strangled cry.)

ARCHBISHOP: Don't give them the satisfaction!

(The GENERAL *freezes, slowly relaxes; breathes, smiles, winks; turns off the running water; walks to the center of the room, turns on the lights, speaks again, for the "record".)*

GENERAL: I'm going to tell you about the drug charges and who killed Hugo Spadafora. I want the lights on so that you can see the smallest lie. Sit down, please, Your Reverence.

ARCHBISHOP: No, I'm tired of sitting. You sit down. I can listen better standing.

GENERAL: I insist, Monsignor.

ARCHBISHOP: I insist. I suffer from the hemorrhoids.

GENERAL: No! Me, too... Here, lie down.

(Bells chime.)

ARCHBISHOP: No...Please it's getting late.

(The GENERAL *puts a pillow down on the* ARCHBISHOP'*s chair. The priest sits and tries to smoke but coughs too violently. The tyrant reaches for the glass of urine.)*

GENERAL: ...That's terrible—I know a cure for smoking. You drink a glass of—

ARCHBISHOP: No, no, never mind. I'm fine.

GENERAL: Here, sit on the pillow. *(Drinks)* Smoking and Hemorrhoids: It is the curse of the intellectuals, it is our "disease"... *(Sadly)* So—after the gold and trees and the cash crops were all used up—there was nothing left except the coca.... The *campesinos* and their coca—and the "War on Drugs". *(He stands on a chair and addresses the "bugs" in the ceiling.)* Now hear this, Operation "Just Cause"! Stop me when I lie, Holiness. Name one lie and I will walk out and surrender to those Green Beanies down there this *minute.*

ARCHBISHOP: Please don't shout.

GENERAL: Your Dignity, we are talking about the "Christians" who shoved opium down the throats of the Chinese people and called it war for "Free Trade"! Because there wasn't enough money—there was never enough money to pay for "Western Civilization"!

ARCHBISHOP: Ancient "History", General.

GENERAL: I am talking, now, Your Excellency, about modern history—*today*—about drugs and guns, about the "Drug Wars"—

ARCHBISHOP: "Supply and Demand" —I know, sir— North America—

GENERAL: No, Father, I am not talking about "Supply and Demand"—I'm going to tell you what the "War on Drugs" *is*! I'm going to give you the "Order of Battle" of the War on Drugs. Are you ready to visit Narcoworld, Nuncio?

ARCHBISHOP: Please sit down, General. You will force them to invade this embassy.... Let us have no provocation, sir. I am too old and you are too shrewd to waste your talents on empty gestures—when both our lives are at stake.

GENERAL: *Both!* You say "both our lives" —because we're in the same boat.

ARCHBISHOP: Yes, sir. The same boat—we are both alone....

(An organ plays, below, in the chapel.)

GENERAL: ..."The Order of Battle of the War on Drugs": forty years ago, when you were a young Priest, the C I A made its deals with the Sicilian Mafia and the Corsican heroin dealers—because they needed an army of thugs to smash the Left-wing unions of France and Italy—and you were there, in Italy, and you know that the Vatican worked with the C I A—you smile—but that's when the drugs started spurting into the arms of the U S—

ARCHBISHOP: In those days, sir, Marxism was the "opium of the people."

GENERAL: Vietnam and the "Golden Triangle" and the heroin flew in on Air America.

ARCHBISHOP: Let's go out on the balcony. We need the air. You're losing your voice.

(The ARCHBISHOP *turns off the lights. They walk out on the balcony.)*

GENERAL: And the Vatican *blessed* the drug trade— because it was the "lesser of two evils."

ARCHBISHOP: What? —Breathe, breathe.

GENERAL: You chose—the Vatican chose to fight Communism with drugs—instead of God.

(A searchlight picks them out on the balcony. The ARCHBISHOP *pulls the* GENERAL *back inside, and closes the drapes over the windows. There is only candlelight now.)*

GENERAL: The Vatican blessed Ronald Reagan's wet dream, the Iran/Contra cocaine connection—Am I right, Padre? After I said no to invading Nicaragua, the U.S. had to do it themselves—and *that* was Iran/Contra, and *that* was how close I came to bringing that crazy cowboy down! Right or wrong?

ARCHBISHOP: *Momentito.*

GENERAL: ...Right now, today, the dope and the junk, the hash and the "horse" is not going to be shot into the veins of the Chinese and the Africans, no, because this is *today*, high noon—the hour of the boomerang. When the chickens and the cocaine come home to roost—when the children of the Empire get *their* fix and go down begging into the gutters, into the sewers,

down into the kingdom of the dead, where I rule
supreme!

ARCHBISHOP: General, we must—

(The GENERAL *takes a candle and leads the* ARCHBISHOP
forward a few steps as if entering into a labyrinth. The
GENERAL *makes the sign of the cross with the candle.)*

GENERAL: Ssh, watch your step, Reverence—I am
leading you down into hell. No, don't hold back, you
asked for the truth, I'm going to show it to you. Step
down, step down carefully, Eminence. Look—you see
there in the darkness, you see it?

(The GENERAL *holds the* ARCHBISHOP *and the two sway
together as if on a ship's deck on the high sea.)*

GENERAL: You see it— "Western Civilization" —you
see it now? The Old World and the New—Europe
and the Americas—the trade routes, see: tobacco and
textiles and tea for opium—opium for slaves, slaves
for rum:—you see your Catholic Church, our mother
church, its martyrs and its missionaries, following in
the wake of the opium trade? Follow me, Father, to
Calcutta and Hong Kong—the brave clipper ships—
white sails, green seas, black skins—and the vast
contraband fortunes of the great families, the royal
families of Europe and the American plutocracy, look
at them: their gold is all gone in their wars and now
"Western Civilization" and the "Church" depends
on the trade routes, the opium roads, the *Camino Real*
binding the Old World and the New, like mother and
child! —Mother and child.... It's a miracle, Nuncio—
alchemy! —You will swear to it, Inquisitor—the opium
trade needs banks and behold: the alchemy of opium
into gold—into *banks!* Banks! London, Paris, Berlin,
New York, Geneva—and now it's our turn here in
Panama, the asshole of the world, it's our turn for our

"economic miracle"—illegal into legal, cocaine into banks, narcobanks, *our* banks!

(The ARCHBISHOP *sinks to his knees; the* GENERAL *kneels alongside him, possessed.)*

GENERAL: No, I told them no, now it's our turn! You can't stop the traffic now just when it's time to turn the cocaine into *our* banks, the law firms, and leisure industries: casinos, resorts, shopping malls, *Disneylands!*

(The GENERAL *roars in mad glee, hugging the* ARCHBISHOP *who has collapsed in his arms.)*

GENERAL: Our turn! We sold our souls, our sisters and our mothers—our sons, and our souls, and now it's our turn—and if George Bush wants a drug war now—in *our* hemisphere—now that he's got *his*—then I swear to you Priest, that the cocaine will go North in body bags from Nicaragua and El Salvador just like the heroin came home from Vietnam, because I can play that game of communists and coke as good as Uncle Sam Bush!

(The GENERAL *rocks and rolls the* ARCHBISHOP *in his arms. Terrified, the priest pretends to expire. The monster straddles him.)*

GENERAL: Shh—wake up, don't die, you got to see the bottom of hell—just a little further, open your eyes—see it, there, look!... The war on drugs is won! Complete victory! Operation "Just Cause" triumphant! See?... But it's not heaven, Nuncio, no, no, it's hell, itself.... No more narcotics and the banks collapse. See the ruins, there, of Citicorp and the Bank of America, I M F and the World Bank itself: no drugs no interest payments—Mexico in chaos, Euro-dollars down the drain, and there's the Vatican's Banco Ambrosiano empty as the tomb of Christ! *(He stands over the priest. He steps into hell, his voice like a drum.)* World

Revolution, Father, seventy-five percent of U S foreign
exchange gone, gone with the stock markets—New
York, London, Tokyo—with the wind—the Fortune
500—without drugs—ghosts, ghouls—no more
Las Vegas or Atlantic City, no Arizona or Florida
or California—the fast track, the limos, the private
schools, the mansions, the health spas—gone—no
more junk no more junk bonds, no more Free Market
no more Free World—no more drugs no more guns,
no more guns no more wars—no more wars no more
capitalism—no more capitalism no more Catholic
church—no more church no more God. *This is hell,
Inquisitor: the war on drugs is won! —And God is dead!*

(The GENERAL *roars and sobs. When the fit passes he
realizes that the* ARCHBISHOP *has fainted. He carries him to
a chair. Soaks the towel and bathes the priest's face until he
recovers consciousness.)*

ARCHBISHOP: ...Thank you, thank you...

GENERAL: Father, you alright? —You're not going to
die on me.

ARCHBISHOP: Yes... Give me a moment... You are not on
drugs yourself?

GENERAL: Never, your Grace... Forgive me, Father, I've
gone crazy. They've driven the whole country crazy....
All of us. Latin America—is the name of a nervous
disease. Did you know that once upon a time I wanted
to be a psychiatrist? Yes, you knew that, you knew....

(The ARCHBISHOP *and thew* GENERAL *breathe. Bells. Sirens
far away. Then they sit at the table. Pause. Outside, at a
much lower level, a voice addresses the troops on the P A.)*

P A: ...5-4-3-2-1-Merry Christmas! *(Cheers, far away)*
...Chow at one hundred hours. *(Then a recording over the
P A of Bing Crosby singing* White Christmas)*

(The GENERAL *goes to the window. The* ARCHBISHOP *swallows a tablet.)*

GENERAL: ...Poor grunts... Bing Crosby... Forgive me, Father. *(He sings along.)*

ARCHBISHOP: General—we only have a few minutes—

GENERAL: Shh—I'll tell you a secret: I went to work for the C I A in 1960. I was just a kid, the "Kid from Terraplan," piss poor and pock-marked worse than now. I won a scholarship to the Military Academy— me and my friend, Hugo Spadafora—and that's when I first went to work for the C I A—and I've been working for them ever since. But you knew that.

ARCHBISHOP: "Co-operating." *(Moving behind the dictator, signaling with the candle, at the draped window, that the beginning of the end is beginning.)*

GENERAL: *(His voice is a choked confession.)* Licking their boots.

ARCHBISHOP: Why?

(The GENERAL *puts the towel over his head as if to hide his shame. The* ARCHBISHOP *peeks under it to communicate.)*

GENERAL: Cleaning up their shit. Pardon me. And you know something? They will wish they had me back—the Yankees—when this new old gang of white tails take over: the *Ribiblancos*—the white men, the comprador class that went to school in the U S— because these traitors will sell drugs for their own profit—not for Panama's—for their own numbered accounts in Switzerland. They will double the traffic! And they will do it for *themselves*. I did it for my *people*, the poor people without shirts—I was like you, I was a diplomat: for the U S, Colombia, United Fruit, the cartels—I set up the Contadora peace talks for them, with the Sandinistas, but the Yankees wanted war, because they're hooked, Washington is hooked on guns and drugs!... George Bush sat in my office three years ago, as close as I'm sitting to you now, and winked at me like an old whore!... Oh yes, Nuncio, they will wish they had their monster back.

ARCHBISHOP: ...The "People"? You did all that for the "people"?

GENERAL: My people, Me I am the people!

ARCHBISHOP: I see.... Well, then your record of, ah, co-operation could help you at your trial. I mean they will all have to testify on your behalf: the C I A, the D E A, the Pentagon—who else? —the Peace Corps!

GENERAL: No. Because I know too much. I scratched their back—the C I A and the D E A—to put the Colombians and the dealers on the spot—I set 'em up—and I let Reagan and Bush run their crazies and their Contras right through Panama City.

ARCHBISHOP: Why?

GENERAL: Why was I a whore for the U S? Why did I help the Yankees make war on the Sandinista Front? Why?

ARCHBISHOP: Why?

(The ARCHBISHOP *and the* GENERAL *are leaning together face to face, talking not for the microphones but for themselves. Pause. The dictator blows out the candles between them leaving only shadows. The priest pants in the close darkness. The* GENERAL *goes to the windows, throws back the drapes. Moonlight pours in. The* GENERAL *sits again, face to face with the inquisitor.)*

GENERAL: Why?... *Money!* Listen: I had a dream! I was head of the National Guard. That means I was in charge of dealing with the drug Cartels. I led them on, and then set them up. You don't understand? No...Father, my plan—and it was working! —was to "launder" all the narco money from Latin America

here in secrecy—to build a banking empire—and I was
doing it, goddamnit! —*I had a dream!*

*(The GENERAL runs out of breath. He lowers his head to the
table. Bells ring.)*

*(The ARCHBISHOP pulls the table out from under the tyrant.
The priest begins his inquisition surgically—his voice and
body now that of the Holy Inquisitor.)*

ARCHBISHOP: ...The money?

GENERAL: Huh?

ARCHBISHOP: No sleeping, now. You did it for the
money?

GENERAL: Like Hong Kong... For the banks... Money...
So we could cut loose.

ARCHBISHOP: From the cartels?

GENERAL: From the U S.

ARCHBISHOP: So you did *not* traffic in narcotics with the
Colombians?

GENERAL: No.

ARCHBISHOP: You just stole their money. Your eye is
twitching, General. You stole the money?

GENERAL: Yes.

ARCHBISHOP: To buy "freedom".

GENERAL: *Exactamente.*

ARCHBISHOP: ...The kid from Terraplen. You.

GENERAL: Me... We took in the Shah of Iran—and the
C I A wanted our doctor to kill him!

ARCHBISHOP: But you refused.

GENERAL: What do you think I am, Father?

ARCHBISHOP: ...Now—the Yankees gave you a new treaty for your canal because they thought you were their "Man in Panama"?

GENERAL: Yes. But I fooled them.

ARCHBISHOP: Did you? You betrayed the Sandinistas as well as the cartels, didn't you? *(He bores in on his victim.)*

GENERAL: You're not coughing, Holiness. I see why they appointed you Grand Inquisitor.

ARCHBISHOP: And the U S armed your National Guard to the teeth.

GENERAL: And taught them how to torture at Fort Bragg.

ARCHBISHOP: You betrayed Fidel Castro?

GENERAL: Yes.

ARCHBISHOP: But you also betrayed the Contras, the O A S, and the U S?

GENERAL: I was a student of Machiavelli, Inquisitor, I was a student of the Jesuits.

ARCHBISHOP: Yes. You wrote a manual on Psychological Warfare.

GENERAL: In high school I dreamed of becoming a psychiatrist—and President of the Republic.

ARCHBISHOP: You dreamed of being him. Simon Bolivar. *(The priest points to the painting of Bolivar.)*

GENERAL: How did you know?

ARCHBISHOP: You wanted to be another "Liberator" of Latin America. Your hands are shaking, sir.

GENERAL: Once upon a time *(A hoarse whisper)* from the Rio Bravo to Patagonia.

ARCHBISHOP: Like Che Guevara.

GENERAL: Che. *There was a saint!*... Did you know him?

ARCHBISHOP: I knew him. *(Makes the sign of the cross)*

GENERAL: After the C I A hunted Che down, we knew the U S would kill everybody if they had to. We were Che's children and we knew that Uncle Sam was a mummy that never slept—they caught Che with a radar that picked up his piss in the jungle! If a man can't piss in the jungle without Uncle Sam catching him with his pants down, then we understood that we would have to get in bed with Uncle Sam first, and then, in the middle of the night when he was all fucked out, then slash his throat!

ARCHBISHOP: So you betrayed both sides.

GENERAL: I betrayed all sided. The Soviets, too. Our banks were "full service": we washed the whole world's dirty money, right here. I was the Priest who "cleansed" the "leper".

ARCHBISHOP: But once upon a time, when you were known as the "Tiger"—

GENERAL: I wanted to be Bolivar!

ARCHBISHOP: Didn't you know that he died sad and mad in his labyrinth?

GENERAL: But that is because he was audacious like me.... During the Reagan regime *everybody* came here to do business. We were Latin America's only successful multinational! And I towered over all the cowboys and Yankees and junkies and Contras and Cubans and dopers and dealers—they crawled between my boots.

ARCHBISHOP: ...You made a bargain with the devil.

GENERAL: With Ronald Wilson Reagan. With George Herbert Walker Bush. You tell me, who is the devil, Monsignor? You're the expert.

ARCHBISHOP: But they beat you. They made the world think you were the devil.

GENERAL: No. I *wanted* to be thought of as Genghis Kahn or Darth Vader, so that—

ARCHBISHOP: Who?

GENERAL: *(Overlapping)* So that they wouldn't know that underneath I was still the kid from Terraplen.

ARCHBISHOP: So you pretended to be a monster?

GENERAL: That's all.

ARCHBISHOP: You put on an act.

GENERAL: I'm an actor. Like you. It was an act.

ARCHBISHOP: A perfect act. You were not a monster?

GENERAL: No.

ARCHBISHOP: You were not Somoza—not Baby Doc— you were a human being.

GENERAL: Well—I would not go that far.

ARCHBISHOP: ...You would not?

GENERAL: No. Not for myself. Not for anyone.

ARCHBISHOP: You would not? I see. You do not think any of us are human?

GENERAL: Not yet. No... Listen, Father, you can see through those who pretend to be saints—and I see through those who claim to be *human beings*. We would make a good team of inquisitors.

ARCHBISHOP: And who killed your friend Hugo Spadafora?

(The GENERAL's laugh freezes, he glares and ends the "confession". Bells. The GENERAL checks the window and the street.)

GENERAL: Christmas Eve is almost over. *(Pause)* What is your verdict? Did I lie to you?

ARCHBISHOP: No.

GENERAL: So you will go to the Spanish Embassy
for me—to the Vatican, to the White House or the
Kremlin—

ARCHBISHOP: No.

GENERAL: Why not? You said yourself that I told the
truth.

ARCHBISHOP: No, that is not what I said.... I said that
you did not lie.... That is not the same as telling the
truth.

GENERAL: Spoken like a Jesuit, Father. Like the Devil's
Advocate.

ARCHBISHOP: Yes.

GENERAL: But you do not follow the "Liberation
Theology" of the revolutionary Jesuits, do you, for
the salvation of the soul and the *body* of the poverty
stricken masses?

ARCHBISHOP: No. I follow the orders of the Holy
Father. *"Perinde ac cadaver."*

(The ARCHBISHOP *lights a cigarette, the* GENERAL *puts it
out.)*

GENERAL: "Like a corpse" ... But you expect me to tell
the truth?

ARCHBISHOP: Yes.

GENERAL: Ha—and "what is truth"?

ARCHBISHOP: You tell me: Why, if you hate the Yankees
so much, you didn't fight them in the swamps as you
vowed to do—why you came here instead—why you
secretly admire them, the Yankees—tell me the truth!

GENERAL: *I hate the U S!*

ARCHBISHOP: Or do you *love* them? Do you? Tell the
truth!

GENERAL: *I'll kill them all!*

ARCHBISHOP: Because they have all the power—all the power—and you were nothing—is that why you loved them?!

GENERAL: *Kill 'em!*

ARCHBISHOP: When—where—how? —You came here. You didn't go to the swamps, did you? You're full of "History," General, but what about the truth?!

GENERAL: *Kill 'em!*

ARCHBISHOP: You came *here*. You came to *me. Why?!* Why—what guilt—what crime?

GENERAL: Why should I tell you—you're not Mother Theresa! You're just the fucking devil's advocate!

ARCHBISHOP: And that's why you're going to tell me! Kill me or tell me—why you came here and what you have to confess!

GENERAL: And then what—you'll save me?!

ARCHBISHOP: No! —Then you will save yourself.

GENERAL: A miracle?

ARCHBISHOP: Of a kind.

GENERAL: No. Miracles are like power, they grow out of the barrel of a gun.

(*The* GENERAL *picks up the gun. The* ARCHBISHOP *moves to confront him.*)

ARCHBISHOP: Is that a quotation from your handbook on psychological warfare?

GENERAL: I see through you. You'll "save" me—if I give myself up. No deal! You're going with me, Advocate.

ARCHBISHOP: Where?

GENERAL: Spain—Rome—Cuba—if I'm the devil then you will be my advocate. To the end.

ARCHBISHOP: No, General...You are not the Devil, finally, and I am not your Advocate.

(The GENERAL *goes to the balcony.)*

GENERAL: If I walk out there and fire one shot—those Yankees will be in here like Cowboys.

ARCHBISHOP: Rome will not permit me, General.

GENERAL: Bishop, you and I know that, Rome, in its time, has permitted everything. *Everything!* Remember Pope Paul? *(Pointing to the photo of Pope)* The man before him? You murdered him.

(The ARCHBISHOP *crosses himself.)*

GENERAL: The Vatican's bankers were swimming in narco money, up to their crucifix, and the new Pope wasn't going for it, and the bankers killed him. And you know it, Excellency, so don't tell me what Rome *permits!*

ARCHBISHOP: You gave me your word—and I hold you to it

GENERAL: That there would be no hostages taken. There won't! You promised me protection and you are going to give it to me—out there in the street!—*of your own free will!*

ARCHBISHOP: I am free—in the sight of God. Not man, General, God!

GENERAL: Listen to me, Padre. I'm not a real General. I'm the kid from Terraplen—the black, brown, yellow, red, white scum of the earth—the scum of the earth, the poor bastards that Christ called the *"salt* of the earth." Christ—remember Christ, Padre, not God—Jesus Christ—flesh and blood! *(He sings out a phrase of the* Misa Campesina, *the mass of the damned, from the Liberation theology. A strangled, haunting melody that pierces the Inquisitor like an arrow.)* "Jesus, O Jesus Christ/Be on our side today..."

(Silence. Wounded, the ARCHBISHOP *bows his head...From below the sound of a mass starting up reaches them.)*

ARCHBISHOP: The last mass of Christmas...I should be there.

(The GENERAL *puts down his gun.)*

GENERAL: You're a free man.

(Slowly, the ARCHBISHOP *turns to leave. The* GENERAL *picks up the gun and puts it to his own head.)*

GENERAL: I am going to kill myself—before they "Neutralize" me.

ARCHBISHOP: *(His voice is a low moan.)* General—stop! You are only a human being, after all. Accept it. Confess it! You are not Adolph Hitler or Joseph Stalin!

GENERAL: I was their lackey, I was their man in Panama.

(The GENERAL *clicks off the gun safety. In the silence the* ARCHBISHOP *hiccups. He sways. He is torn by a dry retch. He knows the* GENERAL *is not bluffing.)*

ARCHBISHOP: Give me the gun... You were the tiger, *el tigre,* remember? You remember everything— remember that! Give it to me.

GENERAL: ...I was a punk for Uncle Sam.

ARCHBISHOP: No—you were *Numero Uno,* the *Commandante Grande! El Jefe!* —I am going, now. Stop bluffing, stop acting.

(The GENERAL's *hatred and self-loathing is fearsome to behold, shaking the* ARCHBISHOP *profoundly, forcing him to gamble for a miracle. He takes a step toward the great sinner.)*

GENERAL: Go!... I was a red-white-and-blue flunky—I was "Pineapple Face"!

ARCHBISHOP: No—you were the "Kid from Terraplen" —hold onto that, sir. Do not do this thing. Suicide is a scandal. It's what they want you to do. Do not give into them, again.

GENERAL: I was George Bush's lick-spittle running dog. I rocked and rolled for Ronald Reagan!

(The GENERAL *cocks the gun. The* ARCHBISHOP *and the* GENERAL *are both shaking.)*

ARCHBISHOP: Then kill me too, because when you shoot yourself, that shot will bring in the marines...I mean it. I do not bluff!

GENERAL: Get out, Father—go to the chapel, they may spare you there.

(The ARCHBISHOP *starts to back away.... In agony, he stops, shakes his head.)*

ARCHBISHOP: No.

GENERAL: Go!

(The ARCHBISHOP *takes a trembling step forward. Walking as if against a gale. Stops. He is ready to die.)*

ARCHBISHOP: I will not leave you. I promised you asylum.

GENERAL: I absolve you! Choose—get out now or come with me as my protector, of *your own free will!*

ARCHBISHOP: No. I have a third choice.

GENERAL: No, you don't!

ARCHBISHOP: I do—because I am ready to die with you!

GENERAL: Jesuit!

ARCHBISHOP: You shut up, now! I am free, I have a third position—I am not a lackey of those people—that

Rock 'n' Roll—I am free! You may not be, you may choose to live and die like a Yankee bootlicker, but I do not! I live and die like a Basque man.

(The ARCHBISHOP *and the* GENERAL *both pant like animals.)*

ARCHBISHOP: Ready?! Ready to die?! I am! *(He begins the prayer for the dying.)*
"Lord, have mercy on him
Christ, have mercy on him
Holy Mary, pray for him
All you holy Angels and Archangels, pray for him..."

GENERAL: Get away!

(The ARCHBISHOP *stalks the tiger, now, in the cage of the room.)*

ARCHBISHOP: "Saint John the Baptist, pray for us
Saint Joseph, pray for us
Saint Peter, pray for us
Saint Paul, pray for us..."

GENERAL: *Stop it—stop torturing me, Inquisitor!*

ARCHBISHOP:
"All you holy Apostles and Evangelists, pray for us
All you holy Innocents, pray for us..."

GENERAL: *(Screaming)* Stop!

ARCHBISHOP:
"All you Holy Virgins and Widows, pray for us
Be merciful to him, spare him O Lord
Be merciful to him, set him free O Lord—"

(The GENERAL *screams in prolonged and hideous pain, hurling the gun away. He arches, leaps, falls, rises. The* ARCHBISHOP's *prayer lashes him like a whip until—the monster rips off his robe and leaps forward to the priest, naked except for his red bikini undershorts.... As the priest prays, the fugitive throws himself into the magic song and*

dance of the Santeria! *The* GENERAL *dances with two
lighted candles, and speaks in tongues, calling out the names
of forbidden gods.)*

GENERAL: *Yaaaa! Eleqqua—Oshun—Obalala—ahaaaah!
Palo Mayombe! Macumba!*

ARCHBISHOP:
"From an evil death, deliver him O Lord
From the pains of hell, deliver us O Lord—"

(The ARCHBISHOP *pulls down the huge medieval crucifix
from the wall and confronts the* GENERAL *as if he were the
devil. The* GENERAL *acts out the tearing off of a chicken's
head and the drinking of the blood, using the towel as a
prop.)*

GENERAL: *Ouimbanda!* Ahh! *Maria de Manta!* Hey-hey-
hey-*hup! Sarava!*

(The ARCHBISHOP *swings the crucifix. The* GENERAL *beats
a samba rhythm on the walls and the furniture as he whirls
away. The moonlight plays over the grotesque ritual. Below,
in the chapel, the worshippers pray and sing.)*

ARCHBISHOP: *(Overlapping)*
"From all evil, deliver him O Lord
From the power of the Devil, deliver him O Lord
Through your cross and passion, deliver him O
    Lord—"

GENERAL: *(Overlapping) Sango! Oba So! Oba Ko So!*
E-yah, e-yah, e-yah—*eeee! Babalawo! Tupinamba!*

(The confrontation reaches its apotheosis.)

ARCHBISHOP: *(Overlapping)*
"Through your Death and Burial, deliver him
O Lord, Through your holy Resurrection, deliver him
O Lord—"

GENERAL: *(Overlapping)* Oshun! Hey-ya, hey-ya, hey-ya—*Spapanan! Shango! Oya! Oshahsee!* Ha-ya-ha-ya—*aieeeee! Candomble!*

ARCHBISHOP: *(Overlapping)*
"Lord have mercy on us
Christ have mercy on us!"

(The ARCHBISHOP *and the* GENERAL *crash together. The candles fall. The men go down in a slow tangle. The victorious inquisitor holds the crucifix high, as in a Picasso tableau, and frozen. Below, the final mass of Christmas comes to an end. Shadows and moonlight.)*

GENERAL: ...Father...I give up...Father...I want to confess...

ARCHBISHOP: You've already confessed too much.

GENERAL: ...But I didn't confess the truth.

ARCHBISHOP: "What is truth?"

GENERAL: The truth is that I knew that the U S was going to murder an honest man, and I didn't warn him.

ARCHBISHOP: ...Doctor Hugo Spadafora.

(In the silence the fan turns overhead like the beating wings of an avenging angel—the ARCHBISHOP *and the* GENERAL *stare up at it.)*

GENERAL: Hugo... He stood up to Reagan. Told him the truth. Told him that his Contras were not Freedom Fighters. Told him that they were a star-spangled death squad.

ARCHBISHOP: Finish it!

(The ARCHBISHOP *sits up on the floor. The* GENERAL *crawls to his knees and makes the sign of the cross.)*

GENERAL: Hear me, Father..."Through my fault, through my fault, through my most grievous fault—I hate the devil, and all his works": I confess to you now the agony and death of the honest mean, my *compadre*, Hugo Spadafora...Friday the Thirteenth of September 1985...Hugo was handsome, women and men loved him, he was bright and white—everything I'm not—his beauty made me more ugly even than I am—maybe that's why I didn't warn him. I don't know. Maybe I loved him.

ARCHBISHOP: Finish it.

GENERAL: ...Maybe I loved him.

ARCHBISHOP: And that makes you afraid?

GENERAL: ...Because he had...everyone loved him...I tried to give him money—he didn't want it—I mean, I would have stepped aside for him but he didn't want the power, either—someone had to take it—the power—didn't they?

ARCHBISHOP: Finish!

GENERAL: They tortured him in the towns of Concepcion and Alaje and near the villages of Santo Tomas and Estero Rico. They murdered him in Corazo at the agricultural station.... In Concepcion they only beat him—rubber hose, rifle butts, kicks, blows—small time stuff.

(The GENERAL *crawls in small circle around the* ARCHBISHOP, *living out, acting out the torture and the agony of Hugo Spadafora. His voice pants, gasps, groans, screams.)*

ARCHBISHOP: Wait, wait.

GENERAL: ...They ran bamboo slivers under his fingernails.... Then they stripped him naked, ah, and made two deep cuts on the inside of each of his legs, ah, so that he, ah, couldn't close his legs when they raped him up the ass, ahh, when they beat him on the testicles, ahh, and tattooed his body with a knife, mm, making the sign of the death squad, ahh, then they plunged a butcher knife into his throat—ahhh! —and cut off his head—

(The GENERAL *rolls in empathetic agony. The* ARCHBISHOP *weeps silently.)*

ARCHBISHOP: I absolve you—

GENERAL: ...They stuffed his body in a U S mail bag, mm, they buried his head in the dirt, mm, and two days later a yellow dog dug it up, mmm mm.... *(He moans softly.)*

ARCHBISHOP: I absolve you.

(The ARCHBISHOP *traces a cross on the* GENERAL'*s forehead. Noreiga suddenly grabs and crushes the advocate's hand.)*

ARCHBISHOP: Ahhh! I absolve you.

GENERAL: You don't! You can't.

ARCHBISHOP: Stop! This is why you really came here, General—isn't it? Not just to save your skin.

(The two antagonists are on their knees, face to face. The tyrant wraps his arms around the priest.)

GENERAL: My pock-marked skin. My leprosy... You can't absolve me, not even the Pope—you're all guilty as hell—Only God, himself, can absolve me! *I dare him to forgive me! (He stares up at God.)*

ARCHBISHOP: *Silence! He cannot hear you!*

GENERAL: *I dare him!*

(The ARCHBISHOP *and the* GENERAL *wait, hoping against hope...but God is silent.... In great pain the* ARCHBISHOP *pulls himself to his feet and limps out to the corridor. He returns with a box. He stands over the broken body of the tyrant.)*

ARCHBISHOP: You did not help your old friend—you did not stop the torture?

GENERAL: No. I was in Paris.

ARCHBISHOP: But the death squad told you everything?

GENERAL: They were my men.

ARCHBISHOP: They belonged to you.

GENERAL: And the C I A.

ARCHBISHOP: You did not give orders for the murder?

GENERAL: No. But I knew.

ARCHBISHOP: And you did not try to stop it.

GENERAL: No.

ARCHBISHOP: The torturers were your monsters?

GENERAL: Mine.

ARCHBISHOP: And whose monster were you?

GENERAL: I don't know...don't know....

ARCHBISHOP: Stand up.

(Bells)

ARCHBISHOP: It's time. You're a clever boy: You remember everything, and you learn nothing. And now it's time. *(He pulls the prisoner to his feet. He wipes his body, including his feet, with a towel.)* I absolve you.

GENERAL: You do?

ARCHBISHOP: I absolve you. But I cannot forgive you. I cannot judge you—and I cannot forgive you.

GENERAL: God.

ARCHBISHOP: *(His voice is a rope of resonance wrapping the prisoner tighter and tighter.)* God... You are in His hands now, son.... When you walk out of here. He will lead you—not to Miami, not to the Yankees, but into the "awful responsibility of time."

(The ARCHBISHOP *finishes wiping clean the* GENERAL's *body. The monster stands like a young boy, even his voice has an adolescent innocence to it.)*

GENERAL: Will He forgive me—God?

(The ARCHBISHOP *now opens the box and takes out the* GENERAL's *full-dress uniform and regalia and begins to carefully dress the prisoner. The inquisitor now uses up the last of his strength. The words he speaks and the way he speaks are a complete contradiction: the tone and pace are contained outrage, and directed at moving the prisoner toward his fate.)*

ARCHBISHOP: ...Of course. When you have suffered. I'm not talking about Miami, Tony, we're talking about God.

(At the ARCHBISHOP's *use of his familiar name, "Tony," the* GENERAL *responds to the diplomat's demands like a good child. The inquisitor helps his victim to stand on a chair.)*

ARCHBISHOP: Step up here, Tonito—slowly. That's a good boy. *(Under his breath)* "Like a cadaver."

GENERAL: Father...

ARCHBISHOP: Turn this way, Tony—so many medals... God will know that you were not a Great Sinner, any more than you were a great man—put this on—that you were no Bolivar, you were not even "Noriega, the narcoterrorist"—turn this way— "terrorism", that's the cheapest word in Latin America—stand by the window, so I can see...Christmas is over.

(The ARCHBISHOP *and the* GENERAL *face the window. Their reflections look back as from a surreal mirror.)*

GENERAL: What happened to me, Father?

ARCHBISHOP: We abused you.... We *made* you—the way the pusher makes the addict.

GENERAL: Who?

(The ARCHBISHOP *cleans the* GENERAL'*s face with a napkin. Both are panting, more dead than alive.)*

ARCHBISHOP: All of us in power. We created you, exactly as the voodoo master reanimates the zombie. We were the true voodoo doctors. In the "cunning of our reason" —Church and State—we sat coolly in Rome and Washington and debated how to manipulate the nigger and the peon and the *mestizos* by using young men on the make like you—perverting their patriotism and belief and hunger so that when the Vatican or the White House proclaimed "Freedom" or the "Holy Ghost", your lips moved like a ventriloquist's dummy. You and your generation of tin pot dictators tortured and terrorized for us—and now you are going to suffer for us—and that is why God is going to redeem you and forgive you, Tony—and one day, you will get your justice. I know—I've seen it all. One day God will come—and He will take the ball— out of our hands—out of the hands—of the terrible players.

(The ARCHBISHOP *and the* GENERAL *stare at each other in the mirror of the window. Below, a P A system gives one sharp squawk, then silence, again. The priest hides the tyrant's gun.)*

GENERAL: ...God?

ARCHBISHOP: Yes, son, God is going to forgive you— because you are going to be tried in Miami—for the *wrong crimes.*

GENERAL: I am?

(The priest has almost completed the costume change, now he must get the monster's shoes on and lace them up as if he were his father.)

ARCHBISHOP: Here—lean against me. You're helping to dress yourself. Such a good boy. Good boy. You never had a chance: you gave food to the poor people and they called you an armed saint, another Che. But when you asked the people why they had no food we called you a terrorist. The rest you brought on yourself, because "you are you".

GENERAL: The new shoes...

ARCHBISHOP: *(Kneeling with shoes, the advocate seethes with self-loathing.)* ...Miami is a dream, Tony, like Panama, a dream and a nightmare—we invented Panama—nineteen hundred and three—as we did Miami, and we moved you through that dream like a sleepwalker, and you never knew who we were, really, or to what end we led you into legend and history— that is what we call Ronald Reagan's comic book, we called it "History." Give me your other one—here— that's a good boy, Tonito.... In Miami, you will wake up from the nightmare that you did not even know you were lost in—stand up, now, son—wake up—*free!*— *Disengaño!*— Disenthralled—suffering—oh yes, Tonito, you will wake up screaming and you will go down in anguish, you will go under for us, for our sins, because we wrote the scenario and your role in it, and you were only human, a child playing soldier's games with the toys we gave you and the slogans we put in your mouth—you will suffer, now, for us because we knew, we always knew, that you were not killing communists for us on the Isthmus— *(Shaking)* You were killing Jesus Christ—for us! And we blessed your troops.... So you see, Tony, your suffering will end some day—*but ours never will!*

(The GENERAL touches the ARCHBISHOP The story has moved the child/monster.)

GENERAL: Poor Father.

ARCHBISHOP: No. We committed crimes against children. We killed Jesus Christ and we used children,

like you, as our instrument. And it was all for nothing:
Because God, He knows everything we did, Tony.

GENERAL: He does?

ARCHBISHOP: Everything. He knows the truth—but he
waits.

GENERAL: Waits...

ARCHBISHOP: God—He sees the truth of our lives—but
he waits.

GENERAL: He's waiting for us?

ARCHBISHOP: You understand. We're not waiting for
Him. He's waiting for us.... Waiting for us to face
the truth of our lives: that we played at being God,
when we were not even men yet, not even human
beings—you said it before, Tony, you understand—
you said that we were all monsters who had called
ourselves men too soon—something like that, you said
something like that. Somehow, all along, you knew in
your heart what we knew in our head— *(Whispers in
the boy's ear)* The Devil.

GENERAL: The Devil?

ARCHBISHOP: We tried to turn you into the Devil. To
fool God. So we could be Gods, too. But God is not
fooled. He knew who the Devil was, all along...I'm
confessing this to you, Tony, because you are going to
see God.

GENERAL: Me?

ARCHBISHOP: You! You're going to see His face. *And I
never will!* Because your only crime is that you killed
the wrong people.... You should have killed us! *(He
puts the* GENERAL's *gold braided cap on him, inspects the
man and the uniform; adjusts, straightens; wipes a tear from
the cheek of the boy, Tony.)* Are you ready, son?

GENERAL: Will you go with me, Father?

ARCHBISHOP: I can't do that. You have to go alone, Tonito.

(*The* GENERAL *begins to whimper.*)

GENERAL: I'm scared.

ARCHBISHOP: No, no, no—listen, Tony, I told you Miami is a dream. You are not going to Miami!

GENERAL: No?

ARCHBISHOP: No. You're going home.

GENERAL: Home?

ARCHBISHOP: Home. Yes. So don't be scared. You're going to suffer, and you're going to be saved.... You believe me?

GENERAL: I do.

ARCHBISHOP: I know.... Stand straight now. Head up. Remember who you are. Say it—"Tony, the kid from Terraplen" say it.

GENERAL: "Tony, the kid from Terraplen."

ARCHBISHOP: That's it!...Follow me now. Come on, Tony. (*The inquisitor leads the monster toward the door.*) Here we go. That's it. That's it.... *Disengaño, disengaño*— wake up, Tony, wake up, son—one—two—three— four. The Father—the Son—and the Holy Ghost!

(*At the door, the* ARCHBISHOP *nods to someone who is waiting. The inquisitor makes the sign of the cross. The* ARCHBISHOP *kisses the* GENERAL, *on the mouth, goodbye. Someone leads the* GENERAL *out and away. The inquisitor crosses himself. The* ARCHBISHOP *halts to the window. Dawn light is breaking. Below the P A system blasts ten seconds of rock'n'roll—then silence. The priest speaks directly up into the "bug" hidden in the fan. His body and voice are wracked with anguish.*)

ARCHBISHOP: ...God forgive us.

(The ARCHBISHOP *returns to where he first prayed, and kneels. The bells toll the hour, the inquisitor's voice rings out as the lights fade.)*

ARCHBISHOP: Lord have mercy on us!
Christ have mercy on us!
Lord have mercy on us!
Christ have mercy on us!

END OF PLAY